The Champion's Choice;

Understanding Christianity

Myles Holmes

The Champion's Choice; Understanding Christianity

Myles Holmes

I remain forever grateful to my precious wife Valerie for her love, her grace, her mothering of our five children and for always being my greatest encouragement. I do not know of a more consistent model of the principles outlined in the following pages than Valerie's sweet Christian lifestyle. XO Forever.

Unless otherwise noted, all scripture is from the New King James version, Thomas Nelson Publishers, Nashville, TN

Myles Holmes Ministries - research@mylesholmes.com

Facebook - Myles Holmes Ministries

Twitter - @PastorMHolmes

Blog – mylesholmes.wordpress.com

Forward

Champions are determined by their choices. In every area of life, every endeavor, whether it is a physical contest, a financial conquest, or an emotional test, the winner is determined by the choices they make. There are no accidental champions; there are no winners by happenstance. Nobody wears the Olympic gold because they were lucky. A dream, followed by a decision, daily disciplines and determination pave the way to victory. Choices.

Spiritually, the process is the same. There are choices that must be made. GOD wants you to be a winner, a champion in this life and the one to come. Jesus said that He came that we might have life and life more abundantly. The Bible says we can enjoy victory that overcomes the world through our faith, and that GOD has made us more than conquerors through the sacrifice of Jesus Christ.

GOD wants us to be prosperous, happy and healthy. Depression, poverty, fear and sickness have never been GOD's plan. He has a much better, achievable plan. However, we must choose. Choose wisely. Choose daily, and choose GOD and His ways, once and for all.

> "Choose for yourselves this day whom you will serve... but as for me and my house we will serve the LORD." Joshua 24:15

> "I call Heaven and earth as witnesses today against you, and have set before you life and death, blessing and cursing, therefore choose life!" Deuteronomy 30:19

This little book is about making the choices that will propel you toward the Champion-Life GOD created you to enjoy. The Greatest Champion, the all-time, undefeated, undisputed champion of life, love, mercy and grace turns it all up-side right. Jesus said, "You did not choose me, but I chose you." John 15:16

Christ has chosen you. The fact that you are reading this book is more evidence that you have been marked. Your best response to His choice is to believe, trust and obey Him. Choose to build your faith. Choose the life of the Champion!

- These messages have been transcribed from live preaching and teaching. We have deliberately chosen not to edit the 'live' feel out of the text. We want you to hear a 'voice', not just read words.
- It has been my practice chosen for decades now, whenever I write and publish, to always present GOD and LORD in all-caps, and satan in lower-case.

Contents

Hope for the Guilty

The guilt had been piling up. It had been years, decades, generations. In fact it had been centuries. For thousands of years, the guilt and shame had been accruing a horrible ledger of debt.

 From Adam and Eve's sin in the Garden of Eden to the lies and murder, hatred and jealousy, lust and adultery, violence, stealing, coveting and greed, anger and idolatry...the guilt kept piling higher. Broken commandments and forgotten vows. Man had lost the way and couldn't find the path back home.

Still, the guilt kept piling on. Sin had been multiplying on top of sin.
Men and women were ferociously inventing new ways to disobey GOD, and even more fervently

trying to discover new ways to hide their sin and shame. But the lingering sense of being lost and alone and far from home could not be shaken.

So we made gods in our own image. We cut down trees and carved them into shapes to worship. We cut stone and rock into images to bow down before. We prayed to gods that have no ears, hoping they would see us with no eyes.

The one and true Living GOD pointed us forward to the only Hope. So, a very special people with a very special covenant and call, were set apart as a nation to love and worship GOD. In obedience to His Word they sacrificed lambs for sin and shame. But even this family could not follow faithfully. The law was a hard taskmaster. They too struggled and failed. They wandered and rebelled. They forgot the GOD who made them. They lost the way home. But GOD never forgot His promise.

Oh, glorious wonder! He promised to come Himself to lead us home! He promised to rescue those who wanted an escape from an eternity of guilt and condemnation. And we find out that this wise and loving and all-knowing GOD, that this was His Plan from the beginning.

He would offer a lamb that was slain from before the foundation of the world, a spotless, sinless sacrifice, the just for the unjust, the innocent for the guilty, Heaven's best for hell's worst, to bring His children home.

And a virgin conceived and bore a Son, born in Bethlehem. Angels announced His arrival. He lived, He loved, He taught, He healed and delivered. He fed the hungry, He showed us how to live. He showed us what our Heavenly Father is like. And we hated Him for it.

So, we led Him to Calvary's altar where another lamb, just another lamb would be sacrificed. But this time was different. Blood flowed, veil torn, the planet shook, graves opened, the sky darkened. Hell must have screamed in terror as Jesus the Christ shouted, "It is finished" and died. And Heaven kissed the sin- stained earth with Mercy and Grace. Oh, Hallelujah what a Savior!

It's now been 2000 years since the Sacrifice for sin was suspended between Heaven and earth on an old rugged Cross. Now, I can't get ahead of myself, it's Good Friday, Jesus died. But in case you haven't heard, He didn't stay dead. Resurrection Sunday morning, history records, the tomb was empty. He rose from death just as He said He would.

So what has changed in the last 2000 years? There is still sin in this world; there is still guilt and shame. There are still millions who walk in broad daylight as if they're in the dark of midnight, lost, hopeless, confused and alone. Still millions who are making gods in their own image, worshiping self and embracing with abandon everything they know deep in their heart is wrong. So what has changed? Oh, my friend everything is different!

There is a way home. Now, there is a way out, and the way out is up. You see, the death of Jesus not only changed life itself, His death also changed death! 2000 years later there now millions who have applied the Blood of Jesus Christ to their guilty, sin- stained hearts, they have believed on

Him and in Him and confessed Him as LORD and Savior.

And Christ has redeemed them, bought them back, forgiven and healed their broken souls. Jesus Christ, the tender surgeon, has taken out the heart of stone and given them a heart of flesh. He's filled up the empty places of the sin-shattered heart with His peace, purpose and passion for life.

He has brought the lost home; given them a brand new spirit that delights in obeying His Word. He's given us a Book to help, guard and guide us. He's given us His Spirit to lead and empower us. He has given us a family, the church, His body to grow in and fellowship with. He's given us the glorious promise and hope that any day now He will return.

So here's the question. Are you one of the healed? Are you one of the rescued? Are you one of the forgiven? Why should you carry the weight of guilt or one more grief or sorrow when He has carried it for us? Why should you be burdened with your sin and failure and inadequacy when He was wounded and bruised for them? Why should you wander through life as if you have no place to belong, when your Father is calling, "Come home, my child, it's time to come home!" The Father is waiting to welcome the prodigals home. Why should you keep on trying to buy peace when He paid for your peace of mind, soul and spirit? It's time to come home.

I Am a Christian

To describe what I am by declaring what I am not, is never very helpful. To say I am not a Buddhist, I am not a Muslim, I am not Hindu, I am not an atheist or agnostic is all true, but only slightly helpful.

It is far more helpful to describe myself to you in terms of a positive choice. However, since there has been so much confusion over my identity, let me continue to clarify.

I am not a Christian by birth. The Christian life is not something passed from one generation to the next by genetic design. I am not a Christian by default. In a multi-ethnic, multi-cultured, pluralistic society, many presume upon the Christian identity simply because they do not plug into any other category very comfortably. That is not accurate.

I am not a Christian by laying claim to any special superiority in morals, character or conduct. There may be moments, or days, or seasons when I am not very kind, or gentle or forgiving. There may be times when I am wrong; dead wrong. I may make wrong choices. I may sin. (But I do have hope about all of that which I will describe later.)

So please, if you think of the term 'Christian' as a label for a self-righteous, religious, pious, stuck-up, gloomy, depressed, angry, holier-than-thou, pharisaical, judgmental, man or woman pointing their bony finger in condemnation at all the low-life... STOP! Understand, that is not a Christian. That is a dangerous religious pretender, a hypocrite, whose bloodline traces and races straight back to their ancestors who crucified the LORD of love on a Roman cross 2000 years ago.

I am a Christian.

I am humbly grateful that I can claim identity with hundreds of millions of people today, from every tribe and culture, red and yellow, black and white, rich and poor. We share a family fellowship with powerful leaders of business and government, humble peasants working the rice fields, hard-working farmers, fishermen and corporate executives.

And we are not alone in time, our heritage traces back to where we have drawn Living Water from the same well of faith that generations before us have. Century after century, Christians have banded together to weather ignorance and intolerance, to suffer persecution and violence. Our history travels all the way back to an empty tomb in a city called Jerusalem in a land called Israel. That geography will help you understand my affinity with the Jewish people, for not only do we share a historic geography; we also share a historical book and a historical faith.

The ancestry of our faith shares Moses, Abraham, Isaac and Jacob, Daniel and Job and Joseph and Elijah. So you will understand why I as a Christian, must pray for the peace of Jerusalem.

I am a Christian not because I am weak of intellect. In fact, like many Christians I struggled and resisted the claims of Christianity. I looked for meaning and hope and purpose everywhere else, but I was continually being drawn by three forces, three persuasions, three convictions.

My intellect was the first. The more I reasoned and researched and studied and thought and pondered, the more curious I became about that Book and soon discovered it to be like no other. Nothing that man has proven historically, scientifically, medically, finds any disagreement within its pages!

I've even found astonishing evidence that the story of creation in Genesis is much easier to believe scientifically than the unfounded theories of evolution. As I studied evolution, I was shocked to realize that Charles Darwin was actually a woman-hating, racist, white-race supremacist. So that helped me understand why Adolf Hitler was so in love with Charles Darwin and his theories, and why Margaret Sanger of Planned Parenthood (who founded PP to diminish the black race in the USA and destroy all the intellectually inferior in America) also was so enamored of Darwin's embrace of white- race supremacy. All of this blatant history is left out of our high school and college textbooks.

Back to the Bible. The history of the life, teachings, miracles, death and resurrection of Jesus Christ are documented by the written records of eyewitnesses. My intellect was heightened by my search for the truth in the story of Christianity.

The second persuasion was my emotions. Now, you can level the charge that my experiences are just emotionalism, but you would have a very weak argument. What human existence or relationship or discovery or need or activity or function does not bring some emotion with it? I don't apologize for the fact that I believe GOD used the emotional needs He placed within me as a human, to help me see my need of supernatural help.

I discovered that I really was not a happy person. I have happy moments. Who doesn't? But I longed for real joy, lasting peace, sustaining comfort, and had tried 1001 pathways to peace and none satisfied. I knew the very fact that I have this inner appetite for something deeper was proof that something deeper must exist.

The third and most intense persuasion was spiritual. That's right, I am a Christian because I believe in the reality of another dimension, another world, invisible to our own, but concurrent with and very much involved with this life.

As a Christian, I believe that there is an eternal/forever part of me that will never die. It's that eternal/ forever part, call it soul or spirit if you want, which is the part of me that has the potential to plug into, or connect with GOD. I resisted this thought with great energy. I certainly didn't want to be counted with the fruitcakes and nut-bars who hear voices and see ghosts, but I could not deny the existence of a spiritual force in my life.

Growing stronger by the day, deep in my gut, was a growing awareness that I was guilty; a sense of condemnation, a sense of responsibility. Some call it conscience, or conviction, I just couldn't shake the knowledge that I was not right. I had a sense that I was wrong. The harder I tried to be good, in my own power, the more I failed and the burden of my own sinfulness and failure only increased.

I'm a Christian today because I've found a way, the only way, the truth and the life. I have found the only way to have this burden of guilt lifted from my life.

I am a Christian because I've been forgiven. I am not better than you, but I'm better than I was, better than I used to be. I know I am forgiven, completely and perfectly cleansed from the responsibility of my sins. Somebody took my place, took my guilt, my shame, stood up for me and took the penalty, paid the price, suffered the judgment, in my place. GOD has pronounced me clean, forgiven and perfect in His sight because of what His Son did for me on a Cross.

Now, you understand my joy, the reason for my smile and my song. Now, perhaps you understand my devotion, affection, love and passion for a Man, a GOD-Man, the Son of Man, the Son of GOD, Jesus Christ.

I am a Christian by faith. I believe the Bible and all its promises. I trust GOD, the Creator of the ends of the earth.

So, I have peace in the midst of the storm. I've got hope even in the face of tragedy. I must forgive my enemies, even love them, because I remember how GOD loves and forgave me, even while I was His enemy.

I am a Christian, not because I read the Bible, go to church and pray. I do those things *because* I am a Christian. I draw life, energy, purpose, meaning and joy from living the Christian life. I've read the research and looked at the stats that prove Bible-reading, church-going, praying people, on average live longer, healthier and enjoy happier marriages than others. That is not why I do it. I live a Christian life by the grace of GOD because I chose to place my life under new management. I have turned over the ownership and management of my life to GOD through His Son Jesus Christ.

We have many terms to describe this Christian experience; Born Again, Saved, Received Christ, becoming a Disciple or Follower of Jesus, making Christ the LORD of my life. All I know is, this process works. The more I trust GOD, believe His Word, act in faith, obey His direction in my life, the more I come to know that it is all true; both by inner conviction and by evidence before me, answered prayers, GOD's help, GOD's presence.

However, I'm not confused. There are some who suggest that we Christians have a faith that works for us, so that makes it true for us. No, Christianity is not true because it works, it works because it **is** the truth. This is a critically important distinction. A drug addict can say his lifestyle is working for him, so it's true enough for him. A Buddhist or a Muslim could say their faith works for them, so that is their truth. Christianity does not offer that level of tolerance. Once again, it is not true because it tends to work, it works because it *is* the truth historically, literally and spiritually. It is the only truth, and the only truth that can set you free.

Despite the joy and purpose and peace I have found in this life in Christ, this is only the beginning. I am going to live forever and forever and forever and way on past that. When I leave this planet by whatever means, by grave or glory- train (that's another story), I will put on a brand-new body, a forever-body, never to be touched by tears or sadness, sickness or loss, pain or despair again. I will be in Heaven, experiencing new joys, new glories, a new kind of work and responsibility, forever with Christ. So, I can make it, knowing my end will be better than my beginning; knowing that it will be worth it all when I see Jesus.

There's so much more I need to tell you, I've only scratched the surface, only skimmed over some highlights.

Guilt speaks to you as loudly as it spoke to me. The cost of ignoring that voice is eternal and unspeakably horrible. Forever separated from God. The only word to describe that is **HELL.**

A strong hunger for deeper reality, meaning, something real, is gnawing at your insides just like it did mine. Why don't you stop running from what you know is true?

Just believe, have faith, turn from yourself and sin and run into the arms of a Risen Savior. He died. He rose again. He's coming back again for me. Will it be for you, too?

Believe, my friend. Trust GOD and GOD alone and then you too, can joyfully declare - "**I am a Christian**!"

WHO IS JESUS?

Jesus paused, put down the sandwich He was eating, turned to his disciples and asked, "What's the talk on the street about me? What's everybody saying?"

And Jesus was not asking because He needed His ego stroked and He needed to see if anybody was getting suspicious that He was somebody special. No, there was no doubting in Jesus mind, exactly Who He was and is. In fact, you will find Him stating over and over again, shockingly intolerant words. You will find Jesus saying things that for any ordinary man we would say his screws are loose, elevator doesn't go all the way up, wonder when he escaped from the asylum?

Jesus Christ had no doubt in His mind as to why He walked the planet. But He was making a point here to the disciples, "Who does the world say I am? What are they saying about me on CNN or

Fox news? How are they talking about me in the halls of Congress? What's the latest scoop on my personality and calling? Who am I to this world?"

They have some answers. "Well, some say you're John the Baptist, back from the dead. Some say you are Elijah. And others say, no, he is Jeremiah, he's back, reincarnated, revisiting the planet. Or one of the other prophets."

And then Jesus asked the question He was leading up to, the question that was really the point of this discussion here. "Who does the world say I am, who does Oprah Winfrey say I am, all the news radio talk shows with their opinions and their experts, and their commentators and their talking heads, who do they say I am?"

Well, they've got some ideas. And then Jesus points His finger at His disciples and at you and me, and every individual on the planet and asks, "But who do you say that I am?" And I want you to sense the finger of Jesus Christ pointing at you right now. I want you to hear the voice of Almighty God through his loving, living, begotten son, Jesus Christ. I want you to sense Him looking you in the eye and asking you pointedly, "Who do you say that I am?"

'Well, my grandmother used to tell me.'

Wait a minute. I am not asking about your grandmother.

'When I was a young boy my mother taught me this song.'

You are evading the question; you've watched too many politicians on television. You answer a question by taking it off track, off stream or going somewhere I'm not asking you to go. I am asking you this question, "Who do you say, **you**, not your mother, not your father, not your neighbor. Who do **you** say that I am?"

What you must understand my friend, is that one day, it may be sooner than later, one day you and I will stand before Almighty God, and the only hope in Heaven that we will have, will be determined by how we answered that direct question, "Who do you say that I am?"

Peter spoke up first because he is just like a lot of us, we like to talk. We love the sound of our own voices. We just love to be heard, because our opinion matters. Sometimes Peter said the stupidest things, just like you and me. Sometimes he would say something and then kick himself thinking, "Why did I say that?" You know, if you open your mouth too quick you're going to say stupid stuff. If you don't stop and think before you speak you are going to eat your words and they won't be like honey.

But this time- this time Peter says something brilliant, something powerful, something that is so authoritative and truthful that it causes Jesus to say, "Hey, you didn't figure this out yourself, you're not smart enough to. You have heard the Voice of Heaven, the Spirit of Heaven revealed this to you."

Here's what's Simon Peter said. "You are the Christ, the Son of the Living God." And Jesus says, "Flesh and blood didn't tell you this Peter, but my Father Who is in Heaven."

You are the Christ, that is Who You are. Peter answered correctly.

You must answer correctly, because there a lot of opinions about Jesus Christ floating around the world today. Some will say, "Listen, he can't be GOD, be reasonable, be logical, use your head. Nobody living on this planet is GOD. He was a great teacher, though."

If I asked how many of you have ever heard that, or perhaps if you've ever said it, I suspect there would be many. But listen to me, Jesus certainly was a wonderful communicator, He spoke like no man has ever spoken before, even His enemies had to give Him that much. They said, "This one, He speaks like one with authority, He doesn't doubt Himself."

Some people talk as if they end every sentence with a question mark.

"My name is Tony? It's nice to meet you? I live in St. Louis?" Everything you ask, even if they are sure of it, they sound uncertain. "What's your name?" "Trevor?" It's as if they're not sure if it's okay. It will be Trevor if it's okay with you, or it seems they are not really sure what's going on.

Not Jesus. There was no doubt, absolutely no doubt. Jesus never spoke questioning, doubting, ending every sentence with a question mark. His enemies could not believe that this carpenter's son spoke with such authority.

Yes, He certainly was a tremendous communicator, a brilliant storyteller and a wonderful teacher but that doesn't tell Who Jesus Christ was and is. Because Hitler was a great communicator! He hypnotized audiences with his oratory and his passion and made people do what they had never dreamed. Hitler was an influencer and a communicator but an intensely evil man. Hitler was a powerful teacher, but a teacher of lies!

If you can satisfy yourself with saying Jesus was simply a great teacher, you are so sadly mistaken, because great teachers would not say things that they could not back up. You see, I could say to you, "I am 6'6" tall!" I could say that with enthusiasm, vitality, great voice inflection and deliver it with passion and great authority.

That would cause you to say, "Pastor Holmes is a pretty good communicator. He delivers with passion, he communicates with a little bit of flair, and is not too boring to listen to compared to some folks, but he's not a great teacher." You would say quite correctly that I am a *false* teacher, not a good teacher.

If I told you the seat you were sitting on was made of cheese, you would say, "He communicates with style and humor, but he has no substance. He's a false teacher, he's a false prophet, and he does not tell the truth."

So, follow my reasoning, you simply cannot say that Jesus was a great teacher unless you believe what He said was actually the truth. Jesus spoke and taught with authority, but if you're not going to believe what He said about Himself, then you have to cross off great teacher from His list of accomplishments. If what He said was not true, then He would be a false teacher, a false prophet, a liar, and not a great teacher.

There are religions in this world such as Islam that say Jesus was wonderful, no one like Him, He was a great prophet in fact, but He was not equal with GOD. The problem you have there is that He said He was, He said that He is.

So, take a minute to think about this. If on one hand you're saying 'He's a great prophet, perhaps the greatest of all prophets, He speaks for God, but He's not GOD', and then you hear what He says, "I and the Father are one. Before Abraham was I AM. I am the Way, the Truth and the Life, no one comes to the Father but by Me.' Now, you've got a problem.

If He is the greatest of all prophets, then He always spoke the truth. If He is not telling the truth, then He's a liar, and He's not a great prophet at all. Not even any kind of a prophet. You see, we are very inconsistent in how we treat Jesus.

Some will say, "Well, he was simply a self-actualized, spiritually evolved person." Some will tell you that we all have the capacity for divinity within us. We can all strive to reach further. Jesus was simply one who reached a little further than all the rest of us. Evolved so far that He said, "If you reject Me you are lost for eternity"? Reached so far that He could go back even before He was born and make sure that He was born of a virgin, and picked the little village He would be born in? That is reaching! That's evolving!

Was Jesus just some more highly evolved, spiritual personality? No. Listen to me, He was the Lamb slain from before the foundation of the world, before you and I were ever thought of, before this world was spoken into being. There sat Jesus at the right Hand of the Father, the Holy Triune God, the Father, the Son and the Holy Spirit. Not three gods, one GOD manifested in three distinct personalities, the Holy Trinity. Jesus was preexistent to all that He created.

Some will say, "He is one of many roads to God. There are many roads to GOD. Buddhists have a road to GOD, and Islam is one road to GOD, and Jesus is just another road to GOD." If Jesus was simply another road to GOD, and there are many roads to GOD, then you would have to disqualify Jesus from being a road to GOD, because He was so intolerant of every other road.

Think of it, Christianity is an intolerant relationship. GOD is a jealous GOD! You cannot worship Jesus Christ on Sunday morning and go to your Buddhist temple on Monday morning and have GOD be okay with the arrangement.

You cannot love Jesus Christ with most of your soul and most of your mind and most of your body but just keep enough so that you can go and worship the devil on Saturday night.

"You will love the Lord your GOD with all your heart, with all your soul, with all your mind, with all your strength, this is the greatest commandment."

And how do you love God? By following Jesus Christ. Jesus said, "You love me by obeying my commandments." So no, Jesus is not one of many roads to GOD. He declared He was the **only** road to GOD. In fact, He declared that every other road is "...a wide road that leads to destruction, but following me is a narrow path, but it leads to eternal life."

There is a very small minority, so small that I hesitate to bring it up, but some say, "Listen, since He said those crazy things, He must be crazy! He must be loony! That's the only logical explanation. Obviously since Jesus wasn't playing with a full deck, the incredible statements that He made, He could not be a great teacher; He could not be a great prophet. He had to be a self-deluded lunatic, a madman."

Are there other people on the planet who declare themselves to be God? There sure are. There are several people in this city with this malady, and we give them medication. I did some prison ministry a while back, preaching to a few hundred inmates, and then we had some time to talk with them. One of them came up to me and said, "You are so pleased to meet me, because I am God." I said, "No, you're not." He said "Yes, I am." I said "No, you're not."

Then I moved away before we had a little altercation and they would not let me come back the next week.

Jesus Christ was not self-deluded, not a madman, not a lunatic. The way He taught, how He ministered, the compassion, the love, the grace that poured from His lips, the authority He spoke with, the self-control that He manifested; all that proved His sanity and intelligence. Jesus had the most perfect, pure mind and intellect that any human has ever exhibited on this planet.

Well, how did He prove that He was GOD? There are a few ways. He proved it with His power. He raised the dead; I'd like to see a madman do that. He opened blind eyes and spoke to storms, "Peace be still" and the winds were quiet. His power proved He is GOD's Son in the flesh.

When John the Baptist saw Jesus coming over the hill, he stopped preaching and declared, "Look! It's the Lamb of God who takes away the sins of the world!" But a couple of years later, we find John in prison because he dared to call the king a bad name. He dared to point out that the king should not be sleeping with a young girl that he is not married to, so they threw him in prison, he is going to die, and he's a bit discouraged.

So he sent some of his messengers to find Jesus to ask Him this question. "Are you the one? Are you the one we've been praying for? Are you really the one that we've been dreaming about? Are you really the one the prophets prophesied would someday come to bear the sins of the world? Was I right when I declared that you are the Son of

God? Find out, ask Him, get Him alone and look Him in the eyes, and say, 'Jesus, are you really The One?' "

So they came to Jesus, and said, "We're a delegation here on behalf of John the Baptist, you know him of course, and he has this question. Are you the One? Are you the One, or do we look for another?"

And Jesus said, "Go and tell John the things that you see and hear. The deaf are hearing, the blind are seeing, the lame are walking, the lepers are being healed, and the poor are having the gospel preached to them. Go back and tell John the things you've seen Me do."

Jesus testified of himself, "The power and authority that I have over disease, over sickness, over infirmities, over demons, over paralysis, over nature proves that I didn't come from this earth, I came from Heaven."

In fact, there were several times when Jesus healed people and He stopped in the middle of the miracle and said, "Now, I am going to heal this person so that you know Who I am. I'm going to heal this person so that you know that I have the power to forgive sins. Rise up and walk!" And they did. Jesus power proved exactly Who He is.

But if we talk about what proves Who Jesus is, you have to look at the prophecies as well. Did anyone write about your birth hundreds of years before you were born? Tell us how you were going to be born? Where you're going to be born, the name of the village? I sincerely doubt it.

The Bible prophesied hundreds of years before Jesus was born, the precise little village where He'd be born; that His mother would be a virgin. That's kind of difficult to predict! Never happened before, has never happened since, will never happen again. The Bible prophesied about His life and His teaching, prophesied specific, minute details about His death and about what would happen after His death. How could this be possible if He were not exactly Who He claimed to be?

How did Jesus prove beyond doubt Who He is? By His power over the greatest enemy that you or I will ever face. You think your neighbor who won't fix his fence is your greatest enemy? You think your mother-in-law who never liked you from the moment you met is your greatest enemy?

No! Your greatest enemy is the last enemy, **death**. You won't escape it. You won't detour around it. You won't take a pass around death.

Someday you are going to breathe your last breath and your heart is going to beat out the last rhythm. Your brain waves are going to be a flat line on the monitor screen in the hospital. Your family will weep and cry tears over your casket. Your body will be laid in the ground. You will be dead and gone.

The last enemy you will face is death. And Jesus grabbed death by the neck, and the Bible says He took the sting out of death! He took the fear out of death. He took out the paralyzing trauma and terror of "Where am I going? How do I get ready? What is happening to me?"

No one talks about these things anymore, but I will tell you the truth. I've stood beside the deathbeds of people who would not repent, who would not get their life right with God, who would not forgive and would not be forgiven. I've seen the ugly claws of death and its stinger take that soul from the body. I felt the cold and the anguish as a person loses consciousness and breathes their last. Monitors flat-line. The end. I've been there.

But, I've also knelt beside beds of believers, of Christians. I've heard the death rattle in their throats, and I sensed angel's wings fluttering nearby. I sensed peace and joy. I've heard them say, "I see Him!" Their eyes were closed but their spirit was open, and they said "I see him!" Who do you see? Who is it?

"I see Him! I see Jesus!"

I have knelt beside them as they breathed their last breath on earth. I've held their hand in mine, and been with their family as they slipped from this existence to the next. But they went on the wings of angels straight into the Presence of GOD.

Now, let me explain why I feel so certain of our safe passage from life, through death, into our eternal existence.

It's like this. Sometimes we tell our kids, "You have to figure this out. I'm not to help you with this math question anymore; I've spent the last week on it!" We don't want to admit that we can't figure it out ourselves. We just tell them, "You will have to work this out yourself. I've cleaned your room up for the last time. I'm not going in there again until you clean it up yourself. If I don't see you until next month, don't come out of there until the room is clean, handle it yourself!"

But have you ever noticed that GOD never says that kind of thing to any of His children, "Fix it yourself!"?

Never once will you hear GOD say, "You've made your bed now sleep in it. You made a mess, fix it yourself." No, instead, He says, "I'm with you, I'm right here. Let Me help!"

And the greatest enemy that we can ever face, the last enemy, that enemy called death, Jesus said, "Wait a minute, hold on, let Me go first!"

He gave Himself, and died in our place to take the sting and the fear and the terror out of death for those who would believe in Him.

The Bible says, "He was the Lamb slain from before the foundation of the world." Make no mistake about it, the sacrifice of Jesus on the Cross was not plan B, was not plan C, was not, 'Whoops, what's happening here? They're going to kill My Son.' No!

Jesus was born of a virgin, lived a sinless life for the express purpose of being the sacrifice for my sins, and your sacrifice for your sins. He was hung up for our hang-ups, stretched out for our stresses, bruised for our brokenness, wounded for our wickedness, striped for our sickness, sorrow and sin, stripped naked before Heaven and earth...and He gave up His spirit. He said, "Don't misunderstand, no one is killing Me, no one takes My life from Me, I give it up." Then He died and was laid in a borrowed tomb; borrowed, because He wouldn't be needing it for long.

Because -

Three days later, on Sunday morning, weeping, mourning, devastated women came to the tomb, crying because every dream they ever had was crushed. Every hope they'd ever realized was demolished. Life was finished. 'But let's anoint His body. Let's make His dead, decaying body smell good as long as we can.'

But He wasn't there! Up from the grave He arose, with a mighty triumph o'er His foes, He arose victorious over death, hell, sin and the grave to prove that He is GOD come in the flesh! To prove that He is the Word made flesh, that He is exactly Who He said He was!

And this teacher- prophet God, this King of Heaven comes to the earth and He points his finger in your face today and He says, "Who do you say that I am?'

Well, my wife says, my grandma says, I read a book once. "No! Who do **you** say that I am?"

You see, unless you confess with your mouth the Lord Jesus Christ, you will not be saved. Not until He hears you answering this query correctly, "Who do you say that I am?"

You see He's interested, here's the kicker right here, this clinches it, Jesus is interested in a **personal relationship** with you. If your mother knows God, Hallelujah! If your sister knows God, Hallelujah!

But He is talking to **you**. Will you confess him? Will you acknowledge Him?

How do you think I would feel, having been married to my sweet Valerie for all these years, if I began to hear that she will not acknowledge that I'm her husband?

Are you married to the pastor?

"Well, that's kind of a private affair. Marriage is a personal issue, it's personal, and it's none of your business."

Well, are you even married, like do you...?

"Look, you're butting in where you're not involved. I told you, it's none of your business!"

Humorous, right? Humorous, but tragic. When Jesus points His finger at you, through my voice, through this message, through the pages of this book, He is asking you, "Who are you to me? Do you know me?"

"Well that's kind of a personal thing, don't you think that's kind of a private affair? I don't wear my religion on my sleeve like some people.

Religion is not something that you talk about publicly, it is just none of your business."

Does that make sense? Less sense than the illustration that I just used about marriage. If you are not willing to confess who Jesus is to you, if you're not willing to acknowledge His presence in your life, to admit that you know Him, and follow Him, then the Bible tells us, that when you stand before Him someday, you will get your way, He will say, "Sorry, I don't believe we've met!"

One more time, I ask you. "Who would you say that Jesus is?"

If you are willing to confess Jesus Christ as LORD and GOD right now, pray this prayer with me. Say it out loud.

"Oh, GOD, give me your mercy because I am a sinner. I have failed and disobeyed You over and over again. I repent. I know I am guilty. Please wash me from my sins in the Blood of Jesus. Make me a new person. Please forgive me. I am sorry for my sins. I repent and renounce all forms of evil, sin, self and satan. I confess, acknowledge and declare that Jesus Christ is my LORD and

Savior, the Living Son of God, who died in my place and rose again to purchase my new life. I will follow and obey You, Jesus. I turn over the ownership and management of my life to you. Fill me with Your Holy Spirit. I want to belong to You forever. I pray this in the Mighty Name of Jesus. Amen.

Welcome to the Family! Now you are ready for the next chapter!

Welcome to the Family!

What Next?

Congratulations! Welcome to the Family of God. What's next?

You have made a decision, a choice. You have determined to become a follower of Jesus Christ. But deep inside you, I know that you have another realization, a growing awareness that this was not simply your decision, you have been drawn to this choice.

There is an unseen Hand that has guided you. Perhaps even over years of your life, your experience, your history, and your past have all played a role, a part in bringing you to this crossroads. All of this helps you know that this is both right and it is real. In fact, Jesus Christ has a word for you right now, "You have not chosen Me, but I have chosen you."

He has had His Hand on you all this time. You see, GOD has had His eye on you for a long time. He has kept you in times of trouble. In fact, I'm pretty sure that you have had times in your life when you shouldn't have made it, it just didn't make sense that you survived, but you did. When you shouldn't have pulled through, when you just missed that car in the intersection, when you have that - "Wow that was close!"- kind of experience. Probably more times than once in your life and those are only the ones you know about, that you're aware of.

So, you have a sense that GOD has been with you, even in the darkest hours of your life. Even in those times you prayed to GOD and you weren't even sure He was there, hoping for His help, and somehow, strangely but strongly, you felt Him near.

We have all taken different paths of course, to get to this moment, to get here; here being a beginning point, a launching pad to a new life with Jesus Christ in the driver's seat. But we've ended up here because of a deep conviction that GOD's Word is the truth, that we have sinned, but we have a Savior in Jesus, that He suffered and died in our place. He paid the penalty, He paid the price for our guilt and then He rose again to prove that He was truly Who He claimed to be, and now He is worthy of my love and adoration, my worship and my service.

I love the writings of CS Lewis. Find any of his books and devour them. He is with the Lord Jesus now, but he wrote; "I believe in Christianity, as I believe that the sun has risen, not only because I see it, but because by it I see everything else." You may want to read that two or three more times and let it sink in. You too, will find that awareness growing in your own life as you follow Christ, as you trust Him, as you obey His Word for your life. By Him, through Him, everything else will be seen in your life. And you will see BEAUTY as never before. Like John Newton wrote in AMAZING GRACE... "I once was blind, but now I see!"

Now, let's anticipate some of the questions that you might ask, or wish somebody might ask in a discussion like this.

What makes Christianity more true than other religions?

The Facts of History. What we believe about Jesus Christ is based upon recorded history. Eyewitnesses who were there, who ate the bread that Jesus multiplied, who saw Him walk on water, who drank the water that had been turned into wine, who talked to the people whose blind eyes were opened. People that were actually there recorded these things. They wrote them down. Eyewitnesses -- that is important to understand -- recorded what they experienced.

If you cannot accept the written record of history concerning Jesus Christ, if you say it's not good enough that eyewitnesses recorded history, then you must throw away anything that you think you know about William Shakespeare, or Julius Caesar, or Cleopatra. Because none of those people had a video crew with them. There's no movie or video footage of those people in history. What we know about them is written down by historians, people that were there, heard them speak and wrote it down.

So, if you reject the Bible because it is an old book of history that happened 2000 years ago, then you cannot believe or trust almost anything past the 20th century when history began to be recorded on video, movies and photographs. Of course, we understand that history can be relied upon and those things that we study in history bring us back to the fact that there were people who were actually **eyewitnesses** of the accounts that were recorded in Scripture.

So, Jesus was not a fable. He was not a myth. The story of Jesus was not a legend passed down from generation to generation, stories around the campfire which somebody wrote down. No, these were the people that were alive, living and breathing, talking to Jesus, eating with Him and walking through town with Him. They experienced these things. They wrote them down while they were alive and if somebody knew that these things were not true, all they had to do was go and open the tomb and show them where the body of Jesus was. These are the actual recorded facts of history. What makes Christianity more true than other religions? Let me give you a second factor.

The second thing we know which makes Christianity more true or reliable than other religions is the Bible itself.

The Bible is the most unique book ever written. It is both the most loved book on the planet and the most hated. More people have died for owning the Bible and reading the Bible than any other book in history. People are willing to give their lives for the pages of this Holy Scripture. There must be something unique about it. It is the most published book, the most translated book, in all of earth's history. You will find the Bible in more languages than any other book. You will find more copies of the Bible than any other book.

The Bible is unique because it was written over a period of 1400 years. No single author wrote it in one afternoon. One author didn't write it over 40 years. 40 different individuals, over 1400 years, some of them kings, some priests. Some were shepherds, prophets, others farmers, some fishermen, and one was a tax collector. All of them, over 1400 years, wrote these pages, and what's absolutely amazing is that there is clarity and unity and verifiable history found from Genesis to Revelation.

That is amazing all by itself. These different people, different trades and different backgrounds, all wrote down some record of history, poems, stories, some ethical teachings, doctrinal teachings, without any disagreement from Genesis to Revelation.

Now, after decades of ministry, I've had literally scores of people come to me and say, "Well, I'd read the Bible, except for all the contradictions." I've had many people say that to me. And in every instance I said, "Well, could you tell me about one of those contradictions?" And every time they say, "Well no, I just heard it was full of contradictions." They have never read it, but they have that interesting, un-informed comment.

Mark Twain was not known for promoting faith, but he had this part down right. He said, "People refuse to read the Bible not because there are contradictions in it, but because it contradicts them and the way they are living." That's why people have trouble with the Bible.

The Bible has a unique character because it is consistent and it is unified. What shows us the Bible's special character, is that it was completed over 1900 years ago, but it has been proven time and time again, to be absolutely trustworthy, right on the mark regarding history, geology, astronomy, biology and medicine.

I guarantee you, today's educators are not using the same science book that you studied in high school, because there are so many new discoveries, so many new observations and facts. "Whoops, that was wrong, we have to put this in here, and well that's not really the way we found it, we have a better microscope now." As a result, so much changes from textbook to textbook, generation to generation.

I guarantee you there will be new medical books out in 10 years that will make some of the things that we presently believe about certain diseases obsolete.

If you have a computer that is five years old, I don't need to tell you, you need a new one now. Things change. But the Bible is absolutely perfect in its origin, and there are so many signs and clues as to its miraculous origin and its miraculous authorship.

Did you know that the Bible says that God sits on the circle of the earth? That's in Isaiah 40:22, written hundreds of years before Christ BC. More than 2500 years ago. And you say, "What's so amazing about that, we know the earth is round?" But they did not know that 2500 years ago!

In fact, 2500 years ago, the accepted idea was that the earth was a flat surface. The Bible says different, and in 1492 they found that out when Columbus sailed the ocean blue.

Columbus is a fascinating character. Our history books today do not tell the story, but he really felt that GOD, in the pages of Scripture, showed him what the earth was all about, and how to get to and fro. Well that is just one, let me give you another.

In Job 26:7 the Bible says, "God hangs the earth upon nothing." We've got astronauts that go out with telescopes and look back to earth and we see that there are no hinges, there are no hooks, no strings hanging, there is nothing holding earth up.

We know that now, but not too long ago they thought differently. Look again at what Job 26:7 says, "God hangs the earth on nothing."

This was written hundreds of years BC, when many thought that the earth sat on the back of a large turtle. That's what their belief system was. That's what the world thought. Other people said the turtle theory was ridiculous, couldn't be true. "That turtle thing is foolish, that's stupid, that's so primitive."

We know the smart Greeks had a much better idea, and said, "The earth sits on Atlas's shoulders, Atlas is holding earth up, not some turtle."

That was the kind of belief system when this part of the Bible was written. GOD, by His Spirit said, "Write this down, I hang the earth upon nothing."

Now, that's just to whet your appetite a little bit. That's just a tease about the kind of things you'll discover in the Bible that were written more than 2000 years ago which prove that whoever wrote this book knew facts about science and about history and about medicine that we are only discovering now. Absolutely fascinating!

So what makes Christianity more true than other religions are the facts of history first of all, secondly, the unique character and content of the Bible which leads us to a suspicion that it must be a miraculous book. It must be inspired by the Holy Spirit. It must be an extremely special book with an extraordinarily special message. We don't find anything wrong with history recorded in the Bible, despite the fact that people have tried to find discrepancies for generations now.

Critics of the trustworthiness of the Bible said for hundreds of years that there was no such person as Pilate. 'That guy in the Bible story, didn't exist- we can't find him anywhere." Then, about 80 years ago archaeologists were just outside Jerusalem, and they were dusting off another piece of rock and guess whose name they found? Pilate!

"Whoops. Okay, you got Pilate." Now, pick somebody else, and over and over again we find the historical records indicate that GOD's Word is absolutely true. Those are powerful testimonies, to the reality of our Christian experience. The facts of history, secondly the Bible, but most importantly is the person of Jesus Christ.

What makes Christianity true? The person of Jesus Christ, His life.

There was no one like Him. He was virgin born. That had never happened before, and it will never happen again. The miracles that He accomplished in front of eyewitnesses, His teachings, even His enemies had to admit no one spoke like Him. He spoke with authority, clarity and purpose. Jesus knew Who He was and what He wanted to say and even His enemies had to admit that they had never heard anyone talk like Him. It was not just what He said, but how He said it.

And then of course, His death. As graphic as the PASSION movie portrayed it, that could only show a fraction. But, please understand that kind of death was not unusual. Thousands of men were crucified under the Roman occupation of the world at that time. It was a gruesome but somewhat common way for a criminal to die. But we do know that Jesus suffered horribly, not just physically, but spiritually, and emotionally more so than any other person. He carried the weight of the sins of the entire world on His shoulders.

Before He even got to the cross, the agonizing torment in the garden was so severe that the Bible says He sweat drops of blood. He was under so much tension, stress and pressure that His body pushed blood out through His sweat glands. The whipping and the crucifixion was a common way to die. And He died. But what was unusual is that it normally took days to die on the cross, sometimes up to a week. It was a strategically designed process of prolonged torture. That's why the soldiers would come around to break their legs so they could no longer breathe or hold their body weight up. Their lungs would then collapse and they would die. But this is interesting; the Bible says Jesus gave up His spirit, after only around six hours on the cross.

Jesus decided when to die. He cried out, "It is finished!" It is paid for!

By the way, the word that Jesus shouted out, "TETELESTAI" is a Greek economic term. It literally means 'a debt is paid for, paid in full, it's accomplished.' 'The sins of the world have been paid for by My death.' Then He died.

He died, but what made His death unusual is that it didn't stick. He rose from the dead three days later, and that again, is recorded by history. More than 11 times that we know about, Jesus appeared to people that knew Him after He was resurrected. One at a time and two at a time. He showed up to 10 at a time, 11 at a time, and in groups of up to 500.

Some people say none of that really happened, it was just a hallucination. I've seen one person at a time have a hallucination, but I've never seen two people have the same hallucination at the same time, much less 500 people. Jesus walked with people, ate with them, talked with them, He really was **really alive**. He ascended to Heaven in front of eyewitnesses, and He has promised to come again.

Those are some of the foundational things that help us to know that Christianity is the truth. Let's have a look now at the personal experience of what happens to an individual.

Second question you may ask. What has happened to me?

'What is going on here? I know something happened. I had an experience, what is this, what happened to me?'

Very good question, answered best by   2
Cor. 5:17. "If anyone is in Christ he is a new creation, old things are passed away, behold all things have become new."

There is a scene in the Bible where Nicodemus came to Jesus and asked, "How can I get to heaven; I want to be sure that when I die I go to heaven." Jesus answered, "You must be born again." And Nicodemus said, "Why would I want to get back in my mother's womb, to be born all over again?"

 Jesus said, "No, I'm talking about being born spiritually, because you need a new beginning, you need a do-over, a second chance, a new life."

We use different terms of course, you've been born again, you have been saved or redeemed.

But to put it into modern language, you have transferred legal ownership of your life over to Almighty God. You could rightly say you're 'Under New Management.' You could hang a sign around your neck, "New Owner/New Management"

Are you different now? Maybe not to look at, but you can expect inner changes of joy, purpose and peace. No more fear of death or life.

I watched a bit of a movie a while back. I cannot recall the movie, so I'm not recommending it, but in the middle of this old black-and-white war movie, was a powerful scene. The pilot was going into his flight formation. He was doing very dangerous things that could perhaps bring him and his whole crew very close to death, and his copilot said to him, "Stop, you're going to kill us all." He said 'I'm not afraid to die!' And his copilot said to him, "You're afraid to live."

Some people are afraid to live, but the entrance of Jesus into your life gives you hope and a future and lets you know that things can be better. You can be saved from the fear of tomorrow, the guilt of the past, saved from the fear of death, and the fear of life, all under GOD's new management!

Are you different now? Yes, because GOD looks at you differently, GOD sees you clean by the Blood of His precious Son. Are you better than other people? No, but you are forgiven, praise GOD! People say, "I have turned over a new leaf." No, you have not turned over a new page, GOD has given you a brand-new **book**, a whole new beginning.

What has happened? Stories often help me. Jesus told stories so often. One of my favorites which helps explain the process of redemption is a story about little Jimmy who went to school one day a hundred years ago in a one-room school house.

He was a poor boy and it had been days since he had anything to eat. He knew better but he stole someone's lunch. He knew he shouldn't but he sure enjoyed it because he was so hungry.

Soon Big John realized that his lunch was missing. He made a scene saying, "Teacher, somebody stole my lunch and whoever did it is going to pay, they're gonna pay big-time because nobody steals my lunch!"

The teacher went around the room and nobody confessed. Finally, the teacher discerned by little Jimmy's trembling lips and tear filled eyes that he was the guilty culprit. The teacher asked, "Jimmy did you take Big John's lunch? You know the punishment; come up here and stretch yourself over this desk." The teacher took out his cane, and said "You know the rules, take off your jacket."

Jimmy said, "No, I can't take off my jacket, sir."

The teacher said, "Take off your jacket now, you stole and you're gonna pay on your back with this cane!"

Jimmy said, "I can't take off my jacket."

So the teacher proceeded to rip his jacket off and suddenly saw why the boy had hesitated. He saw that Jimmy did not want to take his jacket off because he had no shirt on...he had no shirt, no clothes to wear to school, just his ratty old, 2-sizes-too-big jacket.

The teacher stood there, not knowing what to do. The teacher's heart had softened. He couldn't whip this boy on his bare back because he didn't have a lunch to eat, but he also knew that he could lose the discipline, the control of the class. He didn't know what to do.

He decided that he would have to beat little Jimmy, but he would try to make it not hurt too much. So the teacher lifted the cane high but suddenly a bigger hand than his grabbed his arm. He looked up to see that it was Big John who had stopped the punishment in mid-air. John had a hint of a tear in his eye as he said, "You're not going to beat him. You're not gonna hit little Jimmy, you're gonna beat me."

The teacher for a moment was confused and said, "Johnny, I have to punish him, he stole." Then John said, "No, he stole my lunch. So I can take his punishment. Big John said, "Go sit down, Jimmy." Then John took off his jacket, laid over the desk, and the teacher beat the victim of a crime, who took the time, and the pain and the punishment for the little one who should have gotten the beating.

They tell us that from that day on, little Jimmy could never take his eyes off of Big John, his hero, his savior. He loved him, and he followed him wherever he went.

That simple story describes the redemption process. The fact is, we stole GOD's lunch. We sinned. We disobeyed. We have fallen short of the glory of GOD and we deserve to die.

But we felt a Bigger Hand stop the proceedings, and we heard a Voice saying "I'll take the punishment, I'll take the pain. I will die for you."

That's what happened. Praise GOD for our salvation, purchased by the blood sacrifice of the innocent for the guilty, Jesus Christ for we unworthy sinners. Our response as well, is to fall in love with our Hero-Savior.

Another question. What should I do now? What's the next step?

First, I really encourage you to hang out with other believers. Spend a lot of time with people who will build your faith, who will help you to know GOD better.

People are just like elevators, they either take you up or take you down. You know that, from relationships and associations you have. There are people that can lift you and help you, and when you're around them you feel like you can do anything. Then there are other people who will just pull you down.

People will do that to your faith life as well. There are people that will encourage you in your walk with GOD and there are people who will discourage you. You need to be hanging around people that will build your faith life, and lift you up, and the best place to find them of course, is where other believers hang out; at church.

You need to keep the fire burning. A pastor noticed that a Christian man had not been out to church in a while and went to visit him. He said, "We need to see you in church, you need the fellowship, the leaders, you need to build your faith in church." The man said, "I don't need church, my faith is strong, I don't need to go to church to be a Christian."

The pastor didn't say anything at first. He just looked at the fire burning in the fireplace. Eventually he got up and reached with the tongs and pulled out one little log that was burning brightly. He pulled out this flaming log and set it on the hearth in front of the fire.

And the man asked the pastor what he was doing. He said, "Watch how that log burns all by itself." And it was burning, but the flames started to diminish. You know what happened. The flame went out, and then it was smoking and smoldering. The smoke went out, the fire was all gone. And the man said, "I get your point, Pastor."

Together, we burn brightly; we become fuel for one another's faith life. Together, we build one another up, but take me out of the fire, take you out of the fire and we find it's a lot more difficult to burn all by ourselves.

GOD has ordained, GOD has planned that we grow our faith life together. We need to be together because we need to love one another. We need to be in relationship because we need to learn from one another, we need to grow, share and help one another. We need to work in ministry together, we need to find purpose.

Finding purpose.

Everything in your life cries out for a deeper sense of meaning and purpose. In the church which is GOD's Forever-Family, you find yourself being able to connect with a Purpose that is bigger and deeper than yourself.

We can all get excited about something that lasts for five minutes. We get even more excited however, if we find deeper meaning and value and purpose. If we find something that is going to outlast our lives, we have found something that has to do with eternal purposes. There really are only two things that are going to last forever. They are the Word of GOD and people.

So in the church, you connect with people and the Word of GOD, and it becomes a powerfully motivating force in your life to find eternal purposes for which to live.

I like to teach the fact that God wants you to be **totally healthy**. You need a total health focus for your spirit, soul and body. You're more than a body, you know that, but you're not just soul and spirit. Your soul and spirit lives in your body. So

GOD wants you, as long as you're here on this planet, to live in divine health in your spirit, your soul and your body. You can break that down into five basic areas.

Total Health Integration of Spirit, Soul and Body

Building Totally Healthy Lives on the Principles of God's Healing, Restoring Word

- **Foundational Faith... *Spiritual Health**
- **Family & Friends...* Healthy Relationships**
- **Functional Feelings...**
  *Emotional & Mental Health
- **Favorable Finances...**
  *Work + Wisdom + Blessing = Prosperity
- **Fitness and Food...**
  *Nutrition/Exercise/Prevention/Healing

So as you join a church and become part of that family, it is vitally important that you not sit back as an observer. Christianity never works as a spectator sport! Get involved! You need to take part in the worship services, take notes when there is preaching and teaching. You need to learn, and grow together. You need to take part in classes that are available and participate in the fellowship times.

It is so important to get to know people. You do not get to know people by sitting in your church seat being preached at. You get to know one another by hanging out, praying, eating, playing, working, training, learning and growing together. The Bible says the early church met together daily in their homes, breaking bread together, talking together, sharing meals, getting to know one another. That's incredibly nurturing and important.

You also need to be a part of the church because of the service and outreach opportunities that are available. Jesus told His followers to minister to the hurting, to feed the hungry, to help the sick, to clothe the naked, and visit those in prison. Being part of the fellowship of believers allows you to expand and multiply your effectiveness as a minister and follower of Jesus Christ. This is why you have been saved, not just to get you into Heaven but to be a blessing to the world. Join your church and become part of the family.

The next question we are going to look at is; how do I read and understand the Bible?

How do I understand this book written 2000 years ago? The wonderful news is that you don't have to learn how to speak Greek or Hebrew or Aramaic to understand the Bible. Many have done that, and that is wonderful, but today we have the privilege of the Bible being translated into our language, into our common verbiage.

And there are wonderful modern translations. Most often I use the **New King James Version** of the Bible. Many of us were raised with the King James Version. It has wonderful poetic language, it is authoritative, it is beautiful, but we don't talk with all the 'thees and thous, wherefore thou, shouldest, etc,' like we did hundreds of years ago. The New King James Version respects the poetic, lyrical language, it does not change the meaning of words, and it does not reinterpret Scripture, but just brings it into a modern understanding of the way we speak.

We also highly recommend the **New Living Translation**, especially if you are a new reader of the Bible. It is wonderfully helpful to read in the

NLT, in fact that is the translation that we give to new converts. For deeper study, we recommend the **Amplified Bible**.

But for now, let me give you an example of a Scripture that is incredibly important. You really should try to memorize these verses, let me give it to you in the New King James Version and then from the New Living Translation.

Ephesians 2:8 – 10

"For by grace you have been saved through faith, and that not of yourselves. It is the gift of God, not of works, lest anyone should boast. For we are His workmanship, created in Christ Jesus for good works, which GOD prepared beforehand that we should walk in them."

And now in the NLT. "GOD saved you by His special favor when you believed. And you can't take credit for this; it is a gift from GOD. Salvation is not a reward for the good things we've done, so none of us can boast about it. For we are GOD's masterpiece. He has created us anew in Christ Jesus so that we can do the good things He planned for us long ago."

Value these translations. Study from modern translations that can help you get a real grasp on what GOD's Word is saying to you.

It is important to use a dictionary when reading any book. If you don't know what a word means, you look it up. Do the same when you are reading the Bible. If you come across a word or a concept that is unfamiliar to you, look it up in a dictionary.

I also recommend that you start your Bible reading in the book of John, the Gospel of John in the New Testament. It tells the story of Jesus and especially deals with the salvation, regeneration experience. This is where Nicodemus met with Jesus, and Jesus said you must be born again. It talks about walking, living and abiding in the vine, how to stay connected to Jesus. So start reading in John.

Also, let me encourage you that when you are reading the Bible and trying to understand it, and find you need help, ask for help. First, ask the Holy Spirit. He wrote the book, He knows the message He wants you to receive, so every time you open the Bible, every time you get alone with GOD and begin to read the Bible, just let GOD's Word saturate your spirit. Always say, "Holy Spirit, please guide me in wisdom. Teach me." Ask the Holy Spirit for help in understanding the Scripture; it's His book, He lives in you, and He wants to get His book inside of you.

Ask the Holy Spirit to help, but also ask other believers, someone who has been walking with God for some time and who has some wisdom about the Scriptures. Most growing believers would be delighted to share with you what they have learned from the Bible.

Remember what the Ethiopian in the chariot discussed with Philip? Philip asked him, "Do you understand what you're reading". And he said, 'How can I unless someone guide me?"

And Philip was happy to lead him to greater understanding of the Word of GOD, and then to a salvation experience.

So read, understand the Bible, and apply it to your life. It was written for you. People ask me how much they should read in the Bible, I tell them to read enough of the Bible every day, until you have a Word from GOD. That Word might be correction, it might be instruction, and it might be comfort, or counsel, it may be direction for your life. But read enough of the Bible so that you can actually write down, **this** is what God said to me today. This is God's message to me from Holy Scripture.

The next question I want to deal with is this; how do I pray?

Exactly how do I pray? What does it mean to pray? Some people make this so complicated and convoluted. They make it so difficult to pray. But listen, to pray simply means to ask for something earnestly, to sincerely express need or desire.

Not too long ago the word 'pray' was used in the English language between individuals. We would say things like, "I pray you come to my place for dinner tomorrow night.' ' I pray thou loan me thine horse for the evening.' ' I pray thee give me thy daughter's hand in marriage with thy blessing.' Pray was a common word used to express deep desire or invitation. In today's speech we would use the word hope instead, 'I hope'. Or would 'really like.'

So when you pray to GOD, understand that you're talking to a friend. Realize that you're talking to a friend who loves you more than you could possibly imagine. Understand that you are talking to that same friend who has all the resources you'll ever need and wants to help you if you will only ask. That is exactly what prayer is. You are talking to a Friend Who loves you incredibly and Who can meet every one of your needs.

In the Bible, the Greek and Hebrew words for prayer literally mean: 'make a request, to express your hopes, to call on or to call near, to come near to worship, or to bow down before royalty.' When you are praying, you're doing all those things, you are making a request. You're expressing what you hope for to GOD, you're calling on GOD, you're calling on Him to come near, to make Himself known to you. You are coming near to worship Him and to bow down before your King.

Pray simply; a simple, heartfelt prayer, asking GOD for His help. Pray in faith, believe GOD is hearing you and answering you.

Jesus explained it best with this illustration. "If your little boy asks you for a piece of bread, would you give him a stone? If your daughter asks you for an egg, would you give her a snake? How much more will your Heavenly Father give good gifts to those who ask Him?"

Ask in faith, talk to your Friend, talk to GOD in the Name of Jesus, and expect Him to be faithful to His Word. The Bible says that faith is necessary in order to please GOD. As you come to GOD in prayer you must believe that He is, and that He is a rewarder of those who diligently seek Him. So pray simply with your whole heart, believe GOD is hearing you and is meeting your needs.

I have a couple more questions I want to share with you.

How can I be sure that this is not just an emotional response to an emotional experience?

People face this often after a rich experience with GOD, where GOD's Spirit is moving, where people are moved and touched and they respond to a call to make Jesus Christ their Lord and Savior. They have felt and known the Presence and Voice of God, commit themselves, and then later you find that their commitment has diminished. They are not walking with GOD, not serving Him. When talking to them you find they say that they realized that it was just an emotional response, an emotional time, an emotional experience. Some even say they feel like they were emotionally manipulated.

Maybe you're thinking right now about the decision you've made and you're thinking that you are not sure if this was all real. Perhaps it was all emotions; maybe it was just your feelings getting the better of you.

Let me help you and bring you some comfort. Emotions are a fact of life. Emotions are not wrong; emotions in and of themselves are not wrong. However, there are wrong emotions.

Just like food. Food is not wrong, but there are wrong foods. Let me ask you this question. Can you eat too much food? Now, think before you answer. No. You cannot eat too much food, but of course you can eat too much of the wrong foods, right?

You would never point your finger at a person and say that person has eaten far too many apples, far too much broccoli and far, far too many snow peas. Of course not. If someone has eaten too much food, the fact is really, that they have eaten too much of the wrong food.

Emotions are the same; you can't have too much emotion. You **CAN** have too much of the wrong emotion. And it is possible to **display** too much emotion at the wrong time. However, emotions must be based upon truth.

If I knew your best friend's name and I came up to you and looked you in the eye with compassion and said, "I hate to tell you this, I am very sorry, your best friend just died." You, of course would have emotions, you would have strong, negative emotions. If I were to suddenly smirk and smile and say, "I'm just kidding, he didn't die, I am just joking!', you would have instantly different, strong, intensely negative emotions towards me, would you not? You would assume correctly that I was a mean, insensitive, cruel and hurtful person.

On the other hand, if I walked up to you and told you, "We just found somebody's will. Your great, great uncle who you didn't know was a multimillionaire; he died and left you $12 million."

You would have strong, positive emotions, especially if you found out that that was true.

Emotions are not wrong. Emotions are a fact of life. There is absolutely nothing about your human existence that is not attached to emotions. Everything that's happened to you, everything that will happen to you will produce some emotion.

GOD has emotions as well. There are things GOD hates and there are things that GOD loves. GOD is a jealous GOD. There are things that make GOD angry. GOD is a GOD of emotional expression.

You are a human being made in GOD's image, with the ability to feel. Why should it surprise you that GOD would use not only your spiritual needs but also your emotions to bring you closer to Him? Now listen. This is important. Knowledge fueled by emotion equals action. The right information with enough inspiration (we call that 'motivation') can lead to transformation.

The last question I want to share with you is; what can I expect now?

First, don't expect everyone to be enthusiastic about your new life. You will find yourself having different attitudes about things, about life. You will notice that you begin to talk differently, some things that you used to do, you won't want to do anymore. You will have a sharper, clearer sense of right and wrong, not about others, but about yourself. You will be demonstrating new desires, a different set of values, or perhaps you may feel like you have a stronger sense of what's really important.

All of this is happening because the Holy Spirit now lives inside of you. The Bible says that even your body has been created to be the Temple, the House, the Dwelling Place of the Holy Spirit. That living, indwelling Holy Spirit is going to begin to redecorate His House. This will make some people uncomfortable, so don't be surprised by it. In time, many will see that they need not be threatened by your Christian life, you haven't joined a cult, or lost your mind, or been deceived or deluded. They will see that you are now more alive than ever, more at peace than you've ever been, with a greater sense of reality in your life than ever before.

Secondly, you need to also expect your ability to love and to forgive to multiply exponentially. It is a significant mark of true Christian growth that is spoken of by Jesus Christ. He said. "They will know that you are My disciples by how you love one another."

Love and forgiveness marks the Christian in stark contrast to an angry, bitter world looking for revenge and retribution. We are so perfectly loved and forgiven, that we can find GOD's grace to share that love and forgiveness with those around us.

So, I want you to expect that. Expect your ability to forgive to grow, because you have been forgiven. Expect your ability to love and to share love to grow, because you are so perfectly loved.

We say welcome to the Family, friends. It is a wonderful family, made up of hundreds of millions of brothers and sisters around the world today who have met Jesus, and found Him to be the answer to the deepest questions of their hearts. From every tribe, tongue, people and nation, GOD is fueling a holy Revolution of love, grace and mercy based upon the promise that He made to forgive and redeem us, if we only put our faith and trust in the Blood of His Son.

Jesus Christ declared, 'I am the way the truth and the life, no one comes to the Father, except through Me." Now, because He lives, we will live forever, too!

Throughout the eons of ageless eternity, we will enjoy the Glories of His Presence in Heaven, together forever, where sin, shame, hunger, pain and death cannot enter. He promised to wipe every single tear from our eyes.

Until then, let's live, laugh, love and learn together what it means to be truly alive, living the abundant life, the joy- filled life that Jesus Christ purchased for His very own Forever-Family.

The Believer's Creed

By Myles Holmes

"I am a believer.

I believe in Almighty GOD the Father, the Creator of all there is.

I believe in Jesus Christ the LORD, GOD's only Son, born of a virgin womb.

I believe Christ died for me, returned to life, rose to Heaven and is coming back to earth again.

I believe in the Holy Spirit and His power to help me be like Christ and do His work.

I believe the Bible, GOD's Holy Word, and all His promises to me of abundance and eternal life.

I believe in the church, God's Forever- family.

I am the righteousness of GOD in Christ, because I am washed in the Blood of the Lamb, filled with the Spirit, happy, holy, forgiven and free.

I am greatly blessed, highly favored and deeply loved.

I am a believer!"

Final Thoughts on Choice

One of the saddest scriptures in the Bible is Luke 14:18. "They all with one accord began to make excuses!"

The lamest, weakest expression in the English language is -

"I couldn't help it, I couldn't stop myself, I had no control, I had no choice!"

Life is All About Choices

Pessimist says the wind is blowing in the wrong direction.

Optimist says it will switch directions soon.

Realist says readjust the sails, we can use any wind to steer us!

But our world promotes FATALISM instead! Whatever will be, will be.

Forrest Gump's mother was wrong. She thought that, "Life is a box of chocolates, never know what you're gonna get." Wrong.

Life is actually a box of choices, our choice to act and react.

The power of choice is what makes you human!

Animals have instinct. You have a choice!

You cannot choose where or when you are born, who your parents are or how tall you are.

Almost everything else is up to you!

You see, when a person believes they have no choice, they are prone to violence, oppression and depression. They become fatalistic and animalistic. Others are DEISTIC or SATANISTIC, meaning they either blame God or the devil for everything.

Think about it. If everything were up to GOD, if GOD controlled everything, there would be no pain, shame, hurt or hunger in our world.

If everything were up to satan - if satan controlled everything, there would be no beauty, love, joy or faith in our world.

But GOD is waiting to see what YOU will decide! What will you do? What will you choose?

"You are the person who has to decide.

Whether you'll do it or toss it aside;

You are the person who makes up your mind.

Whether you'll lead or will linger behind.

Whether you'll try for the goal that's afar,

Or just be contented to stay where you are."

Edgar Guest

Joshua 24:15 ...Choose today whom you will serve...but as for me and my house, we will serve the LORD!

Myles and Valerie Holmes have been married and in ministry together since 1983. They have traveled in preaching and music ministry throughout the USA, Canada, the Caribbean, and into China, Israel and South America. Their Christian television ministry on various networks has blessed the Kingdom.

Their 3-fold passion is to win the lost, bless and build the church and encourage other ministries.

They have 5 adult children, all married and serving God, spread from British Columbia, Canada, to Dallas, Tulsa and Illinois.

Myles and Valerie have pastored a wonderful church called REVIVE, just 12 miles east of St. Louis since 2010.

Contact them today for prayer or a ministry booking at office@reviveusa.net

Made in the USA
Lexington, KY
18 May 2019